Coronavirus and The Movement:

TO THE CHURCH AND ALL HUMANKIND

It's Time to Fix It

Joanna Walker-McClain

Copyright © 2023 **Quiet Whisper of Jesus Publishing**

All rights reserved. No part of this publication may be reproduced, distributed, or transmitted in any form or by any means, including photocopying, recording, or other electronic or mechanical methods, without the prior written permission of the publisher, except in the case of brief quotations embodied in critical reviews and certain other noncommercial uses permitted by copyright law. For permission requests, write to the publisher, addressed "Attention: Book Rights and Permission," at the address below.

Published in the United States of America

ISBN 978-1-960684-99-8 (SC)
ISBN 978-1-960684-98-1 (Ebook)

Quiet Whisper of Jesus Publishing
257 Windigrove Dr. Apt 1505
Waynesboro VA 22890 USA
jamaicangal43@aol.com

Order Information and Rights Permission:

Quantity sales. Special discounts might be available on quantity purchases by corporations, associations, and others. For details, contact the publisher at the address above.

For Book Rights Adaptation and other Rights Permission. Call us at toll-free 1-888-945-8513 or send us an email at admin@stellarliterary.com.

The coronavirus has no respect for who you are. It is moving at a faster rate than we can talk. It started out slow and rapidly increased into every part of the earth. It's no respecter of persons, and God is no respecter of persons. The coronavirus is not concerned with whom it takes out as it does not know color, race, or ethnicity. It only knows the air. The prince of the air is in the earth more than ever, and while you are fighting vertically and horizontally, it's springing through the air, discreetly taking out more lives than you can possibly think or imagine. While the crime on hate and violence is being talked up and spreading, the coronavirus is going at a faster rate than the Washington march of the Black Lives Matter movement is.

The coronavirus is the reciprocal of what you are seeing in the movement. Two movements—one visible, one invisible. No cure for coronavirus, and the cure or vaccine that is found is of no assurance that it will work. The coronavirus is taking lives more than the guns and talk of the earth situations are. The coronavirus is taking center stage while the Black Lives Matter movement is still on the move to solution. Both seek attention and solutions, but one has a great solution—humans. "If my people, which are called by my name, shall humble themselves, and pray, and seek my face, and turn from their wicked ways; then will I hear from heaven, and will forgive their sin, and heal their land" (2 Chronicles 7:14). Each race has to put down the obvious and seek the *solver*, the *solution*, the *remedy*, and the *redeemer* that can change and transform lives into greater vessels for his greater glory. God wants a person unto him whom he can use for a purpose, a task, and a mission. Each race has to understand that there is a bigger fight and that it can be healed with love, forgive- ness, and humility. When each race understands that they need one another to make it work, the coronavirus will become at a standstill. The greatest cure to human is love—when one attributes love, that attribute shows God. "God is love, and He who dwelleth in love abideth in God, and God in Him" (1 John 4:16). When one is fighting for their lives and there is no cure to give—give love; give God—this is where the church comes in to speak a word to heal, deliver, and save. The world needs saving, but if the church is adding to the flame, it only makes it worse and leaves no door for God to go in. But where the church begins to pray, really pray for change—God can come and heal. The land is crying for healing; whom can God send, whom can he call on to go and deliver a word to a dying world? While Black and White people are fighting, the coronavirus is killing.

"The thief comes to kill, steal, and destroy" (John 10:10). While the movement is happening, the coronavirus is sweeping through, stealing lives off the operating table, out of the homes, and killing lives (there is no place it respects; it does not matter where you are), and destroying families and their homes. Is the Black Lives Matter movement the important factor today? No, it's not. It's the lives that are leaving us—with helplessness from the government, the nurses out on the front line doing all they can—but the coronavirus does not care who it hurts; all it does is to carry out its plan. But this dis- ease can be healed if we first heal a nation of a sin that has polluted the country too long—the riot, the hatred, and beating up on one another. Stop for a second and think, "If I shift my focus, what is left? What is left is the issue at hand: the disease. Then what I can do apart from staying apart, as staying apart is still not helping anyway, is to pray, fast, and pray."

"Some things only come out by prayer and fasting" (Mark 9:29). We can save the rest of the lives by taking an inventory of our lives and the other lives that are fighting to live, and we can start uniting ourselves to fight, to bring the nation back to prayer, to bring the nation back to love and go about our business without others mingling, and to have a sense of freeness so each life can impact another. Then our dual purpose and focus will be back on God, our Creator, the only one who can save this land from the coronavirus. The coronavirus has no power greater than God, but for God to answer, we have to bombard heaven with fasting and prayer and a true heart of repentance.

The Lord has left us ways to heal the land, and the first is turning back to him so he can heal the bodies he made. "We are His people and the sheep of His pastures" (Psalm 100:3). He made us, so he and only he has the true cure to heal a dying world that he already died for.

We don't need people to be dying without a reason, but let God return to our country, back into the hearts and souls of his people. The people of creation and the land will impact the coronavirus; lives will see the hand of God move. Unity brings and gets the heart of God. He said he made us to be one. In oneness, God will *always* show up, but he has to be invited in.

The Black Lives Matter movement only exposed the country for what it is, exposed the church to where they are, and caused the coronavirus to enter the backdoor and destroy and take lives that should still be here with us. This movement distracted the people, had them out in the cold, and in the cold, the coronavirus came in and conquered through the disease. United we stand, and divided we fall. The devil only needs an open door or a vessel to work through, and he uses the two most popular races to take out loved ones, take out every one of all walks of life—children left us, Black lives left us, White lives left us, young and old left us, experienced workers on the front line left us, and the coronavirus is still on the move. Because it does not see color or even gender, it came as a pollution and polluted, divided us six feet away and conquered. The coronavirus is a spirit, and it did what no other lethal weapon could do in a short time—to disrupt the entire earth, not just one nation, not two or three—it touched the entire world and showed out. It showed that it had more power than did the church, which should be praying and seeking God's solutions and answer to destroy this weapon against humanity. "The weapons of our warfare are not carnal but are mighty through God through the pulling down of strong holds" (2 Corinthians 10:4). This disease can only be conquered with God leading us and showing us how to pray. Instead, the churches were closed due to mandatory regulations from the government. This was the time for the church to stand, rise to the occasion, and be like Daniel, "Don't punish us all, give me time to pray, and I'll be back with the answer." Daniel took his prayer warriors/prayer partners and prayed until God answered. Then Daniel returned the next day to the king with the answer, and what Daniel did was to bless God. He said, "Blessed be God who showed what this dream of the king is" (Daniel 2:20–23). Daniel and the three Hebrew intercessors saved them and everyone in the land from being destroyed by the king. When the king signed a decree, it was a sign; it was a done deal. But when you are in God, you can ask for time to go pray and overturn the king's decree. Daniel prayed, and God answered. Just like today, the church had the opportunity to pray, seek God, and petition the president for the time before he shut the whole country down.

It was God's finest hour to shine, but the church took a back seat to the six-feet-apart rule, to the shutdown, and to the mask. Government representatives before they had a government shut- down: Washington will meet to pass a bill and stay on it until it was feasible to pass to avoid a shutdown. What if the church were that relentless to say we are going into the temple to pray and praise God, and we are not coming out until we get an answer for the president, the country, for the nation's lives are at stake and we need to hear from God. We need a word from God. If we don't hear from you, Lord, what are we going to do? Because "without vision, the people perish" (Proverbs 29:18). Lord, we need to know what to do as the entire country is at stake and lives are dying, being lost, and not even sure they got the chance to know you. Lord, this is on us to show the world that you can heal and do the impossible, to let the world know your power still flows and is stronger than ever to meet coronavirus and put it in its place.

Daniel prayed, and God showed him the dream of the king and the interpretation to the dream. God knows the seed to the corona- virus and can destroy the coronavirus because he made the body, and if you are a believer, the body is the temple of the Holy Ghost, so when the coronavirus meets the holy vessel, the coronavirus has to bow because, "at the name of Jesus, every knee must bow and every tongue must confess that he is Lord" (Philippians 2:10).

The coronavirus can't speak, but we can testify that God can destroy the coronavirus and send that spirit back to the pits of hell, from whence it came. The church is in its finest hour and can still be if the church truly begins to pray. Let's move out—shift out the Black Lives Matter movement, shift in God—love, and see our land heal again. Let's teach and send the right message, and let's drive out hatred because that's the bottom line to both race and hatred—hatred kills; the fruit of the flesh kills and shows the heart of man. Let's start sending the right message: love. Let's turn the other cheek, and let God take care of it all. He is the *master* with the plan. Could it be that we placed so much emphasis on this that we missed God in the process? He's the *solution*. Call on him, and he'll hear, and he'll heal. Don't be angry or jealous when the wicked prosper in their ways. Fear God and live.

Let's turn our eyes on Jesus, and let's serve him, please him, and the rest he'll take care of, and you'll see a fruitful land. Nothing goes unnoticed before God. Bring the nation back with the right words with teaching, and fix a land that is emotionally dying, spiritually dying, and economically changing—everything is flowing in the wrong direction. Teach love, and a heart for God will heal all these emotions, cause the spirit to flow in God's way, and it will bring the economy back—because people will give again. Giving heals, and giving causes people to do great things.

Take the people back to the altar, take the problem back to the altar, take the nation back to the altar. God will take it and use it and give us something better. Let's first kill it all—fix it, fix it with love.

The coronavirus is a call to *repentance* and a call back to God. When the people pray, God listens. He hears and does great things. It's time for the church to wake up, arise to duty, arise to the true call in this hour—saving lives. Millions of lives are at stake, and the church can save plenty. God can see into where we can't. It's time for the government to let the church do what only the church can do through God: heal the people. It's time for Blacks and Whites to see God and seek God and turn from the hatred and crime to love and happiness and trust to each other. It's time for a nation to honor God again and put God back into the things they always have—in God we trust. Let's trust God to do the impossible. Trust him with our lives, money, relationships, and all the ships that we'll have. He'll take us safely home.

Flowing in the Spirit

Flowing in the Spirit causes one not to lose sight of what God wants and his intention for his people. He's a God who never lies, and when he promises us something, he always comes through on his promises. He seeks for a nation that will worship him, people who will be and are sold out to him, so he can continue to reign and use his people for his divine will and purpose. Isn't that what he wants us to do anyway? He said he will send us out, "Go ye therefore and teach all nations baptizing them in the name of the Father and of the son and of the Blessed Holy Ghost" (Matthew 28:19). God calls for a nation that will turn to him in the midst of a crisis or when all things are flowing great.

God is looking for his people to remember that he is God and, besides him, there is no other. God is calling for his people to call on him, for he is near and he is always near to those who call upon him. The days ahead are numbered, and he is the only one who can take us through the uncertainty and the things that will fall in the way that are not foreseeable. God is calling for a nation under God to remember he sees all things, knows all things, and is ever present. There is nothing that can befall us at any time and overtake when he is the *author* and *finisher* of our *faith*.

God seeks for such one who will worship. A worshipper remembers that there is nothing that God cannot do. A worship- per remembers that God may not come when they want him to but that he's always on time, and a worshipper stands still and knows that he is God and watches God in his finest hour. When we follow hard after God, he'll show us things to come. He said, "I will not let anything come up on us unaware," and nothing will he do before he first reveals it to his prophets. Is there a prophet in the land who can stand and decree what God is saying to the nation, to the people, to the church before it befalls us? Is there a voice in the land who will say, "Use me, Lord, to send forth your Word. Use me, Lord, to stand upon the watch and be a voice in these end-times"? Is there a person who will say, "Lord, I avail myself to prayer, to worship, to praise, to keep in tune to you, and to speak for you"? Isaiah said, "Send me, Lord, I will go" (Isaiah 6:8). Jesus said, "I will go down and die for Adam's fallen race."

If you see in the Old Testament, there was one who said "Send me, Lord" when the Lord said he was looking for a voice. In the New Testament, Jesus said, "I'll go down and die for Adam's fallen race." After he left, he said to Peter, "Feed my sheep." As you see, there was a voice in every hour, in every era, or in the time when God needed a voice. Who will say in this hour, this era, "Use me, Lord, for thy glory"? If we look at the signs of times and look at what is happening in this time, we have approached a different era in life, one when we need to look at and say, "Lord, use me for thy glory."

In the month of August 2020, the Lord came unto me as he ministered and said, "I am looking for an army, an army that will stand in this hour and echo a sound that only comes from him, a sound that will change things around us, a sound that, when others hear, they know it's a call of God. A people that won't compromise but decree what God is saying to his people and watch upon the watch." As he continued to minister to me, he talked about Mary; the angel visited Mary and said, "Blessed art thou among women, blessed and highly favored" (Luke 1:28). The angel continued to tell Mary that she shall bring forth a child and she shall call his name, Jesus, for he shall save his people from their sins.

Mary said, "Be it unto me, Lord, according to thy will." Mary accepted the call of God to bring forth the Messiah (which, at that time, she did not know, but Anna and Zachariah stood in the temple, believing that the Messiah would come). In that era and time, the land needed a change, and a quick change they knew was that, if Jesus stepped foot into the world, humanity would be saved, a change would come into their land, and the Jews would be exposed to the Messiah they were told was coming and hoping to come (even though, when he showed up, they gave him much grief, but that did not stop the Lord from fulfilling his promise and what he came to do). Who will take up that torch and run for God and speak for God even if the world gives them grief?

In each era, God had or has a voice that will not be tired to speak and talk for God, one who will remain in his presence, in tune to him to lead and minister to the people. God is using the things that are happening in the earth to show that he needs an army, an army in the White House, to fight for the people and deliver to the people that which is good for them, to give to the people when they need it the most, not to hold back from them since they have plowed into the economy and the things that made the economy great, whether they are unemployed as they have worked and helped the economy in the time they did or never worked a day in their life, because their purpose is greater than the natural work, yet they are useful to the economy, the country, and the people they know. A government that will work for the people and by the people. They won't shortcut the people to delay things that are of greater importance: fighting for the economy and fighting for the country. People who will stand for what's right and give due justice to all. When it really matters, it's the time when the government needs to shine. Whether they have to work countless nights to pass a law or a decision made, this is when it matters for the people and by the people. The people need the government to stand every time, but the greatest message of saying "We are standing with you" is when the people need it the most or need you the most.

Don't be the lawmakers who deliberately do things to make a name or to deny and abort, but be a government that deliberately will make things right for the country that you serve because it's in those times the people see your heart and your intentions. You really want to make the people understand the government? Stand for them when it's the time, and they will stand behind the country's laws and principles all the time. They will remember the work that you did that went a long way. Government members of the house, what's your purpose? Then, what's your human purpose? Who are you standing for, and why? Are you standing for *justice*? Justice, then, is doing what's right no matter what. Do you love the people you serve, or are you just opposing the people sitting across you? Those are not who really matter; it is the ones who are out there in the workforce and those families at home depending on them. It is the ones fighting overseas for the safety and the good of the country, and they have families and loved ones at home praying that they return to them. It is the students getting education and looking for a brighter future. It's the ones you don't know are working behind the scenes and all the working people and nonworkers. These are the lives that really matter.

Not just one issue, but humanity is what matters. If you take the oath to serve the people and be there for the people, serve them every time you walk through the doors to make a decision or make a law. What would you do or feel if you were in their shoes? Don't get up to make it hard for the people; get up to make it safe and easy for the people such that, at the end of the day, you can say, "I did what my hands were assigned to do. I am pleased in the laws that were made today and the decisions that were passed." Let God be proud at the end of each of your day.

If you should stand before him right now, can He say "I am pleased that the law did not make you or your peers change you but you changed the law. You made it better for my people to live in the world to call their place home, and everyone is happy with what you do"? He is changing not only the ways of government but also the church. It's time for the church to stand and pray more in this hour. It's the finest hour of the church to tell the world that we know a God who can do all things and not fail, a God of love and peace, a God who can take a bad situation and make it good.

This that is written is a concern to the heart of God. It has come up in the nostrils of God, and it's something that he wanted to address. There is a greater fight in the earthly realm, and the church has missed the fight. The focus on the Black Lives Matter movement has become a concern to God, and here is God's response.

It was September of 2020 when God started to answer some questions about the movement and gave me a message one Sunday morning regarding the issues that the earth is facing. Before he starts giving me answers, he causes me to come into connection with a book. It's disturbed heaven, first of all, because of the place it came from. We, the church, allow one situation to publish a book that should have been dealt with in the church among believers, among the saints, or in private with both parties who are/were having the issue. The matters of the church should be taken care of within the scope of the church. As the Lord says in the Bible, you should not take your brother to law. In this book, one can rebut that it was not taken to law, but for it to be published such that everyone can read it, it may be concluded that the world knows about the matters that should have been dealt with in the church. The news reporters and journalists can write about a matter, but the matter is delicate and should have taken care of with that network or the church. The Lord starts to deal with me on the matter of this book and how it opens up so many doors that should not have been opened. It added to the issue rather than fan away the issue.

The Lord shows that: does one's race matter? All lives matter. We allow one race issue to pollute our world, society, and the world. It's a war that should not be fought in the manner it has been fought. If his life matters and he died for us, what about your life? "If a man should seek to keep his life, he shall lose it but if he shall lose his life for His name's sake, he shall find it" (Matthew 16:25). God wants us to fight and live the good fight and life of faith that will cause circumstances to bow at the God we serve and will cause love to drive out or cast out fear. "Perfect love cast out all fears" (1 John 4:18). Love is the key to disband disunity and bring the people together. Paul talks about love and put it in a way that all who reads can under- stand. A powerful fruit that will sustain and maintain humanity in oneness because love is God, and ye who dwells in love abide in God and God in Him. Paul defines love with the spiritual/Christian principle in 1 Corinthians 13:3–7:

> Charity suffereth long, and is kind; charity envieth not; charity vaunted not itself, is not puffed up. Doth not behave itself unseemly, seek not her own, is not easily provoked, thinketh no evil; Rejoices not in iniquity, but rejoice in the truth, bear all things, believeth all things; endureth all things. If we keep the unity of love among all men we will win the war against humanity, love conquers all.

That's the fight he calls us to fight. If the church stands in this hour and stands in prayer to God, the world can be healed, and the church can be the church.

The Black Lives Matter movement has shifted the country's focus and has caused a distraction in the world. It's become headlines when there is a greater fight, the coronavirus fight. This virus has killed more Black lives than it has killed White lives and is still taking lives off the earth. If we have a movement that says "Let's save more lives from coronavirus, and let's pray and send prayer cloths and oils to homes so that bodies can be healed faster," our focus on the movement will become vague and not all on this matter.

God wants us as a nation to shift back our focus. Everyone look into the mirror and ask yourself, "Does my life matter? My life matters." In the same breath, say "Everyone's lives matters." There will be a bond of unity because, believe it or not, these marches are building hate, resentment, and killing. Hate kills people and stirs up strife. The Bible says, "Thou shall not kill" (Exodus 20:13) and "thou shall not bear false witness against thy neighbor" (Exodus 20:16). If the Bible says "Thou shall not kill or bear false witness," it means you shall not. If the White lives understand that there is a greater fight than that of their race, they can see Blacks the same. The question becomes whose lives matter: is it that only Black lives matter? Is it that only White lives matter?

These two races have lost themselves in themselves and their race and forgot that there is a bigger world out there than just their race. What is the fight about? Are we trying to repeat history or leave a legacy? Are we trying to get there to raise media attention, or should it be the virus? But at the same time of the spread of the virus, the movement was there and the virus is wiping out not only Black lives, but White lives, as well. This virus is taking both races, and one doesn't see what's taking place. We have placed the camera on Black and White people, and because we have stood long and hard to make a statement, this virus came for months later after the book was published and started wiping out everyone, Black and White the most. Then the cry for children was heard, and the virus started taking out the children.

The Lord wants us to stop taking the Black Lives Matter movement to the extreme and start looking at each other's lives—does your life matter? So does everyone else's. So if you are Black, there is a bigger world than the Black race; if you are White, the same. Understand there are Hispanic lives, Jewish lives, Islamic lives, and so many more lives all over the world. God wants this movement to cease and return to understanding that, Blacks, if you are being fought this much, maybe you should start thinking differently and try to understand why the Whites fight the race—there's potential. Can it be they are jealous of you and threatened by what you may become and do if you are turned loose? Can it be that they know no better and feel the earth belongs to them, when, in reality, "the earth is the Lord's and the fullness thereof, the world and they that dwell therein. For He had founded it upon the sea and established it upon the floods. Who shall ascend into the hills of the Lord, or who shall stand in His holy place? He that has clean hands and a pure heart who has not lifted up his soul unto vanity nor sworn deceitfully. He shall receive a blessing from the Lord and righteousness from the God of His salvation" (Psalm 24). Blacks, review and answer. If you are not able to find the answer, pray, but don't retaliate because the world sees you one way. Prove them wrong; better yet—stand out, and if you are a believer, stand for God. He'll fight for you.

Whites—what's the real deal—are Blacks really disturbing to you, or is it that you that don't think they belong in your world? Are they the inferior one, or is it you inferior to the Blacks? Until you find the true answer, you'll keep fighting a race made by God. He made both races, and the race today is not who is better than the other—the race is eternal life. We must work to get to glory and enter in the end. We must work to see our Lord in the end. If we keep fighting the wrong fight, you are only killing that which has a heart, a soul, and a person who is good in the eyes of God. He said we "are fearfully and wonderfully made." So let's review what the fight is about. Jesus came and died for you and me. He did not just die for the Blacks (as the Word says, his features were those of a Black descent). He did not die for just one race. He did not die just for the Jews, but for all *mankind*. In his eyes, there are two races, Jews and Gentiles. You are either saved or not saved, a sinner. Which one are you? Which of these races are you from? Because by grace are we saved through faith and not of ourselves, it is the gift of God. We are chosen by God to live. He gave us a choice, to choose life or death— he wants us to choose life.

"Black lives matter" is a saying that has caused a riot in the country, and the world and has woken up dead wounds. If people of the world see one another through the lenses of God, one will under- stand that every life matters. Let not our new president have to come and fight a race or humanity battle when Christ gave his life for all. If you are saying your life matters— God knows; that's why he came. If his opinion does not outweigh man's opinion, then your focus is man's acceptance. But if you understand your worth, your value, your appreciation, you won't let the media get the best of you on the riot train to prove your point. You'll rise to make a change.

I came here in 2000 and went to pretty much an all-White school and landed in a community where it looked like Whites were in power. I remembered because it was so new, not much familiarity like that where I came from. Adjusting in the first semester was challenging, but that summer, I said to myself, "I am a child of God, and I am not going to be afraid of their faces when God lives in me. So if they don't like me, too bad, because Christ was not liked by every- one. And if we were liked by everyone, then something is wrong." I took that charge myself and changed my senior year. I remembered comments like "Is this the same girl in junior year?" "Didn't know that you had a big mouth?" For me, I only speak when it makes sense or I have something to say impressing on me from the Holy Spirit. Sometimes, there are some things you need not respond to if they're of no value. As the Lord talks about conversation, how to act, and ask questions, I took the Word of God and live accordingly, day by day—it's my compass and my road map to success. If we walk in the Word, we only deliver the fruits of the Holy Spirit, and we change the things around us. We refrain from unnecessary combat and conflict we don't entertain. When we walk in the Word, we will not fulfill anything of the flesh or the lust of the flesh. We know how to treat each man and how to answer every man. So during my first week of senior year, I addressed what needed to be addressed. I remembered hearing "Who are you?" My stand in God and not letting the looks of faces caused me not to live in their world but to take a stand and respond, "You didn't give me a chance, you just judged me from what I look liked."

People of all races, God did not call us to be inferior especially when we belong to him and are of the household of faith, but instead, he called us to be examples—good examples. Don't add to the flame; be a flame fanner, and fan things away. If only the church can rise and say there's a better way and promise that God will make it all right. Can it be that we are missing those legends of faith and believers who many have gone home to glory (Jen and Paul Crouch, Bishop Patterson, Billy Graham, and others) or the songwriters and singers who are here with us and whose songs are not being played like they used to be played over the air, people like Pastor Shirley Caesars, Pastor Donnie McClurkin, Yolanda Adams, psalmist Judy Jacobs, the prophet Juanita Bynum, CeCe Winans, Mary Mary, to name a few, and the worship leaders? Are we playing more of the new artists that we missed or shifted the church to a new era when these songwriters and singers spent years in the Lord's presence? They get these songs downloaded, and you know they are anointed songs because they pave the way. And when you listen to them, they were and are on time, set the pace for the week, the day, going to work or just home, working and worshipping and dancing and enjoying the Lord. These songs open up the presence and fill your cars with joy, with the anointing meeting the anointing, and you get lost in the presence, perfumed by the glory of Jesus the everlasting king— Shekinah Glory.

When we omit this foundational music, we don't let the new generation hear about in the way that is breathtaking. David said, "Let one generation praise thee to the next generation, that he goes onto say, He'll tell His generation and they will tell their generation until all have heard about God" (Psalm 145:4). It was important in David's time that God was told to every generation and that they carry on the foundation of what they heard and how it was built. Maybe the earth is missing that perfume of music that kept the generation for years. When these are played, these are music and thanksgiving into the ears of God and causes God to give his ear to hear the sound that humanity is making unto him. This kind of music and worship draws the heart of God, and he hears and answers. It helps to sanctify the earth with the right perfume that opens up the presence of God over the earth and will control and keep down world issues. Now there are more world issues and nation issues, and these have taken center stage while God has taken backstage.

With the coronavirus, the church has accepted the nation's call, and no one fights to keep the church doors open to invite people to go for prayer, get healed, and stay healed. It was a time for the church to rise and ask for reconsideration to have the country open because we have the answer—Jesus. He's the *healer*. To have them go to their church, where they'll be prayed over and they'll be healed. That's what God said, "If any is sick among you, let them call for the elders of the church, they shall lay hands on the sick, and they shall recover, and their prayers shall save the sick" (James 5:14). It was the hour of faith to meet science, which has no solution quick enough to execute, and the immediate remedy was placed on hold—going to the churches and being healed. Churches were closed due to the six-feet- apart rule, a measurement that is always used mostly at funerals—six men carrying you back to the preacher, graves six feet deep.

We have missed the real fight—to fight off the coronavirus and coming together. The coronavirus divided the land and placed the world into a place where people are away from one another while it is open to riot Black lives. May Black lives never look at their lives as insignificant—but go forth and live by prayer, faith, and the Word. May White lives look at the whole picture that their lives matter, and one race should not be so important as to stop them, to fight and eliminate them. But may both races be like the characters in *Facing the Giants*—one team looks weak at the last game but, with God, is the strongest—*or* take on the characters of those in *Remember the Titans*—Black and White. The old nation should watch these movies again because there's a strong message of God in both movies. In *Facing the Giants*, one White coach was looked down on by his own race, but with prayer and seeking, God prepared him for victory, and God was there. In *Remember the Titans*, there were Black and White coaches, but the greatest message apart from the team coming together is the White coach's submission to the end of the game (the game to end the season). When he asked the Black coach for help, he showed humility, and after the game, he said he knew football when he saw football, and he applauded the Black coach for what he did to the team. Football for them was not the game but what was done to get them in the game and to the end of the game. They won over all.

This nation is a nation going in the wrong direction because it is fighting the wrong fight. Look in the mirror, then look at one another and tear down the walls of insecurity, envy, strife, and jealousy. When the elements of hatred are eliminated, there is no movement but a life of love and peace in God. This can only be done when everyone says, "Lord, show me the way. Teach me, help me, and allow me to be an example everywhere I go. Everyone's lives matter." Let the church be the church, set the first example, apologize, live right, and God will do the rest. God can heal and want to heal and restore if we will let Him. As we are in the end times, it's the time when the church have to pray the more as the Lord instruct us to pray without ceasing and also to watch as well as pray (1 Thessalonians 5:17 and Mark 13:32–37). If we stay on watch, God will take us through live hurdles and battles and show us the way because He is the way and knows the way. Time to pray.

Let God do it.
Let God be God.
Remove from the movement into your place in him, and watch him heal the land.

Presidential Election 2020

This election is one that is a mandate and call for a time such as this. This election is one of God's interventions in the earthly realm. A change needs to take place in the government, the people, and the nation. The entire world needs a change. God's heart has been pricked, and this situation at this time is what it is. This situation and all situations can be changed if you let God do what he alone can do. Be it known it was God, and if you didn't see God in it, look again—put it on replay. Months or a month before the big day, the new president-elect was seen as weak, feeble, not capable, inadequate, one who didn't have a clue, and all the negative connotations and salutations he could be given were given. He was despised and rejected by the Trump team and all who were against his running, but in the moments of truth, you see the man who was standing tall, standing to stand in the eyes of the people. As it got closer to time, Biden became more and more clear that he was the man with the plan and able to take the country to the next step. God gleaned on him, shined on him, and his (God's) character radiated more and more. His attributes came showing on election night.

Even though the election took days and had delays in adding the ballots, it was a time for God to prepare the people for what was to come. Moments of anticipation and excitement rose as the days of ballot counting continued. The reporters were excited and intrigued at the process while the news company stations waited in anticipation and awe of what was taking place—a change in ruling in some states was about to make history. Things were turning more than was seen in decades, and the reports, ballots counters, news-covering team, campaign teams, the nation, and the world waited in anticipation. This was happening; it was taking place, and it was about to happen—Biden was about to win and was taking over and creeping in. And the news finally came: Biden was announced the next president. The nation and the world are celebrating—change has come—it has come, and the world feels it. At the night of his speech, one could see he was ready and equipped, full of God's joy and excitement to take the country out of the current economic situation and emotional downturn to a more peaceful, celebrating, joyful nation. He was full of things ready to make the change. God came through and showed that Biden is the man of the hour. The hour of newness, the hour of hope, and the hour of us making it is back, and the nation is looking brighter than before. God steps in. It looked dark until the unveiling of the president; light had shone again in America. God was speaking to the people, "I hid him until it's time to reveal him." The people mocked him, they talked badly about him, but at the finest hour, God showed up and exposed both characters: Trump was petty and not ready; Biden, equipped and fully loaded for the task at hand.

It's when you look the smallest in the enemy's eyes that God is getting ready for a blow and to make a name. He's going to move. It's when the enemy is trying everything to cover the hour and evil has risen against you—look at what God is going to do against your enemies; it's the hour that will show the world what he has been doing. The presidential debate was the moment of unveiling to the American people who President Trump really was and would be if he got one more term—demanding, controlling, and not human- friendly. Biden was calm, cool, and collected. His manners and demeanor came through, and his true character came forth. He's the one that is fit for the people and to make a change. Trump is a name for himself; Biden is all about the people being better—rebuilding and having a sense of hope. Who would you want to look out for you: the one about himself or the one all about you? You rather should choose the one who is about you. They'll put your needs above theirs and make sure that the country is taken care of in the best way possible. If you should lose your name for the Lord's sake, you'll find it in the end. The days of a dark spirit hovering over the land are about to move, and the hate in the people that rose and caused sickness to be higher than normal and everyone fighting their brothers about Black Lives Matter seemed to lessen on November 7, 2020. With such an emphasis and a media coverage, the movement turned the focus to one race, and they have been the spotlight; but if we remove the spotlight and say everyone's lives matter, the world would be a better place. One is trying to repeat history when you have made that part of history—make another statement that we've come through the Cold War, the Civil War, the movie *Remember the Titans*, and let's learn from these and not go back. Going back is going back to hate, hate crimes, violence, and slaying and killing of not just of Black lives but of every life in the way. Children are suffering, women are feeling the heat, and men are dying. Is this the way we want our children and the next generation to remember us, or do we want them to remember us with the legacy that we do everything we can to make peace and live peaceably with all men? We are for everyone, and we are for God. Through a legacy of how to live, to be, and to move and with the legacy of Jesus Christ, we can make it through each day.

The president has work to do, but God has already graced him for what is to come. He'll make history again and make God proud. There may be things from Abraham Lincoln and other legacy presidents that may not have been fulfilled or may need to be expanded on, and this presidential team will be able to achieve and complete the task at hand. He will change the generation and all generations to come, and the words "In God we trust" won't be just mere words that are a part of our daily lives; people will know to trust God and call on him for everything. The church and the state will have their platform, and one won't stand in the way of the other because that's how it was built by the Founding Fathers, who trusted God in all things and built a country with meaning and a lifetime of legacy to pass down to from generations to generations. David said in his writing in Psalms that his generation shall tell the next generations and that they'll tell their generation of God so that all generations shall know God and live for God and walk for him, that they will experience the blessings of God in every way. People see America as the land of prosperity and opportunity and a place to get ahead and make dreams come true. It all happened when the Founding Fathers made sure that "In God we trust" was on their money and things of meaning and of value—*family*, *education*, *government*, *politics*, and everything had its place and knew in God we trust. Saying "God bless America" was not just a saying to the Founding Fathers and members of faith. When the church says "God bless America," they mean it from their hearts, and when the entirety of America says "God bless America," this saying goes to another level because the young, as well as the old, get to pray the same words, and the saved and the unsaved are saying the same thing—"God bless America." There is reverence for God. To some, that's their prayer for a long time and probably will be for another long time; but in the moment of saying these words, everyone just prayed to God, and God blessed America. America remains blessed because these words were not just words to God; these were prayer requests from all the Americans and others who say "God bless America." Those three words are powerful in the ears of God and send a message to heaven that signifies, "God, we are asking you to bless America. Don't leave it unprotected or unprovided for, but in each day, bless America." Those words have hit the heart of God, and he honors the *faith* that comes with these words. We are asking you, Lord, to remember us, cover us, and protect us. As I am typing "God bless America," I feel the sweet Lord revealing what these words are and mean every time he hears them. It is people saying "Remember us, Lord," and though the words may be three, God is on assignment on these words. Heaven heard and answered. God is revealing to me in this moment of typing this book that these words hold values and are of power because the entire nation believes in their *country,* and the only time that they all agree is when they say "God bless America."

But when they take God out of schools and consider the idea of taking him off the money, the country starts becoming blind and not being able to run its democracy or people or the currency. They start to slip and look one way, but the acknowledging of God and him being in the place he should be causes the country to be blessed. This goes for everything. When we put God first and serve him, he'll make sure everything is good and great. He'll take us through everything while blessing us in every way. America's trust in God has preserved America's land and people and became a vision for other countries to be and modeled. America is a place that God can bless again with the right people in office. Let the church arise in this hour for God, both the states and the country.

Biden is the right president for the hour who will destroy the wrong look at the presidency and rise the right teams over the land to take up the shield the right way. With the joy back in the country and the new light dawning in on November 7, 2020, when God steps in, everyone has a different view on life, have a pep in their steps, vacations will be great again, and it's sweet to look forward to the plane rides, bus-tour rides, train rides—just the journeys, the trips, and just enjoying every moment of vacations in the places that call history. Visiting historical places will become lively again, and different travel destinations will restore excitement and joy, full of love and laughter.

God intents us to enjoy every waking day that he bless us with all of the possibilities because each day is unique. "No two days are the same or should be the same. He did not intend for that, but morning by morning, new mercy we see" (Lamentations 3:22–23). Whatever God gives us each day, he gives us that for a reason. Enjoy each day with full appreciation, and let him lead us each day into green pastures, but know all things are meant for a purpose and for a reason. There are blessings in each day: look small, and you'll see big; look through God's eyes, and you'll see him move in every way for you. Pray, believe, seek him, and enjoy the manifold blessings each day.

November 7, 2020, was a new day marked in the country and the world. The world was waiting to hear and see the results. A turning happened in November 2020, new things were born, and the heavens were opened over and upon us. If you were looking into the blessings of the day, God was speaking, and he was saying a lot. The right people in leadership yield the blessings of God. Wrong leadership yields nothing but the opposite and confusion. You'll know them by their fruit. God stopped the bleeding on November 7, 2020, and placed a man who loves him—you can tell by his behavior. When Saul takes kingship (understand the Israelites cried for a king, and God gave them Saul), he began to rule but got his eyes off the mission and started to place focus on himself after David defeated Goliath and destroyed the Philistine's attack on the Israelites that he became jealous of David's victory. He was no longer for the people but for himself and looking great. He could not deal with the people chant about David's victory and saying Saul kills his thousands and David his ten thousands. David was for God, and being for God, he was able to care for the people as he has done all his life, living, taking care of the sheep. David was on an assignment even with the sheep, and then God took him, anoint him, and eventually made him king to lead the people. If we take the word of God and input it into what we saw in the election and after the election, Trump rose up as the people's choice and eventually made it about him, while Biden fought to take the people out of the all the crises that are facing the country. When you are chosen by God, the people's needs are going to be one's top priority because that's the heart of God. It takes having the heart of God to lead in any battle and to lead a people to victory. With the heart of God, one will know how to move each day. God will endows with power from on high to carry out the task ahead. Whomever God chooses accepts because they'll bring what God desires for the hour and the people and the kingdom of God. Blessings follow whomever God appoints.

Just like Esther, it was the hour for her to stand for her people, and she was among those women who wanted to have that moment with the king. It was in those times of spending with the ointment and perfume to get ready to go before the king that the sounds and cries of the people were pressing on her heart, and it was when Mordecai revealed to her that, if there was anyone who could change it for the people, it was her because God was giving her favor with the king. Esther took the hour of appointment to see the king and make it a request time to free her people from being killed. God allows and opens the doors to opportunity for us to make a change, make a difference, and stand out. Will we take those moments? President Joe Biden has America in his heart, and he ran for the presidency to make a change.

May our lives be with purpose for God and in God. May we shine each day to make a difference and be a difference. May we impact lives from all walks of life and show the true meaning of *brother* and *sisterhood*. May God be pleased with our every move in him and for him, and may we live each day to make him proud.

About the Author

Joanna Walker-McClain, the mouthpiece of God that only speaks for God when he says and how he says. She is not the one that will speak of herself, but she lets the Lord speaks for her and about her. All she wants the world to know is that God got something to say to his people, to the world, and the generations to come. If we open up, we'll hear him speak in this hour and louder in some things if we care to listen and are listening. He died and does not plan to die again, but for the church to rise and stand in this hour, in his hour, and stand the test of times. Her biography is God's biography of what he wants to say to this world. He writes her life, and about the author, is that her name is Joanna Walker-McClain, speaking for her Master. Will we listen to what he has to say? So much he has to say to the body of his and to the world at large. Give him a chance to really speak, and change is inevitable.

Author of the Lord Jesus Christ and our soon-coming king, a messenger to the people—the church and all humankind. I am Joanna Walker-McClain, and this is from the heart of God. All the glory and praise go to him. Let's hear what God is saying and fix it.

Printed by Libri Plureos GmbH in Hamburg, Germany